PRESENTED TO Jen

FROM Benson

JOHN C. MAXWELL

THE

JOURNEY

FROM

SUCCESS

TO

SIGNIFICANCE

NASHVILLE, TENNESSEE

Published by the J. Countryman division of the Thomas Nelson Book Group, Nashville, Tennessee 37214.

The New King James Version (NKJV) ©1979, 1980, 1982, 1992, Thomas Nelson, Inc., Publisher.

Design: Lookout Design Group, Minneapolis, Minnesota
Cover Photo: Daryl Benson/Masterfile

Published in association with Yates & Yates, LLP, Literary Agents, Orange, California.

www.thomasnelson.com
www.jcountryman.com

www.injoy.com

ISBN: 1-4041-0111-X

Printed and bound in the United States of America

INTRODUCTION

WHEN YOU ARE EIGHTY OR NINETY, and you're sitting on the porch rocking and looking back on your life, how will you feel about it? You won't have to answer to anyone or fulfill their expectations —not your parents or your business associates or your spouse. What will you have done with the gift of life? The answer will be important to you then, so the question should be important to you now.

The course of your life is determined by . . .

~THE RELATIONSHIPS YOU FORM
~THE DECISIONS YOU MAKE
~THE ACTIONS YOU TAKE

Each has the potential to change the course of your life.

If you're *not* doing something with your life, it doesn't matter how long it is. If you *are* doing something with your life, it doesn't matter how long it is. Life does not consist of years lived, but of its usefulness. Your focus must be *beyond yourself*. If you are giving, loving, serving, helping, encouraging, and adding value to others, you are living a useful life. That is significance.

GET
BEYOND
YOURSELF

SUCCESS is when I
add value to MYSELF.
SIGNIFICANCE is when I
add value to OTHERS.

—JOHN C. MAXWELL

> as long as leaders worry
> about who sits at the head table,
> they have little time
> for the people
> they are called to serve.
> we don't see opportunities
> for service
> while our eyes are fixed on
> the competition.
>
> —C. GENE WILKES

THIS IS THE TRUE JOY OF LIFE, the being used for

a purpose recognized by yourself as a mighty one; the

being a force of nature instead of a feverish, selfish

clod of ailments and grievances complaining that the

world will not devote itself to making you happy.

I am of the opinion that my life belongs to the whole

community, and as long as I live it is my privilege to

do for it whatever I can. I want to be thoroughly used

up when I die, for the harder I work the more I live.

I rejoice in life for its own sake. Life is no brief

candle to me. It is a sort of splendid torch which

I have got hold of for the moment, and I want to

make it burn as brightly as possible before handing

it on to future generations.

— GEORGE BERNARD SHAW

———— " ————

IT's easy to make a buck.

It's a lot tougher to make a difference.

—TOM BROKAW

———— " ————

Many persons have the wrong idea

of what constitutes happiness.

It is not attained through self-gratification

but through fidelity to a worthy purpose.

—HELEN KELLER

PERSONAL PERSPECTIVE

ONE EVENING AT SAGAMORE HILL, President
Theodore Roosevelt's home in New York, naturalist
William Beebe walked outside with his host. Roosevelt
searched the star-filled night sky and, finding a small
glow below the corner of the constellation Pegasus,
he said, "This is the spiral galaxy Andromeda. It is as
large as our Milky Way. It consists of one hundred
billion suns. It is one of a hundred billion galaxies."
Then Roosevelt looked at Beebe and said, "Now, I think
we are small enough! Let's go to bed."

— " —

A certain authority attaches to all leaders,
and leadership would be impossible without it....
Leaders have power, but power is safe only in the
hands of those who humble themselves to serve.

—JOHN R.W. STOTT

— " —

i believe that it is not dying

that people are afraid of. something else.

something more unsettling and more tragic

than dying frightens us. we're afraid of never having

lived. of coming to the end of our days

with the sense that we were never really alive.

That we never figured out what life was for.

— HAROLD KUSHNER

shun those studies in which the work

that results dies with the worker.

— LEONARDO DA VINCI

——————| " |——————

The thing is to understand myself,

to see what god really wishes me to do . . .

to find the idea for which I can live and die.

— SØREN KIERKEGAARD

——————| " |——————

DOING NOTHING FOR OTHERS is the undoing of

one's self. We must be purposely kind and generous, or

we miss the best part of existence. The heart that goes out

of itself gets large and full of joy. This is the great secret

of the inner life. We do ourselves the most good doing

something for others.

— HORACE MANN

——— | " | ———

show me a man who cannot bother
to do little things and I'll show you a man
who cannot be trusted to do big things.

— L A W R E N C E   D .   B E L L

——— | " | ———

ultimately we do everything for one of two reasons:
To serve ourselves, or to serve God.

The man who keeps busy helping the man below him
won't have time to envy the man above him.

— H E N R I E T T A   M E A R S

The high destiny of the individual
is to serve rather than to rule.

—ALBERT EINSTEIN

A GREAT man is always
willing to be LITTLE.

HIS LIFE WAS HIS MASTERPIECE

THE MOVIE *Mr. Holland's Opus* was written by screenwriter Patrick Sheane Duncan, who came up with the idea one day while struck in a traffic jam. He heard a news report on the radio about the cutback in school programs and the number of teachers in the state of California.

"Suddenly I realized how important my own teachers had been in my life," says Duncan, "and that the most important thing we can do as adults is educate our children."

Duncan remembered the one special teacher who made a difference in his life. "She was reputed to be the meanest and toughest teacher at my junior high," he recalls. "But she was the one who bought me my books and gave me her own son's clothes after he'd grown out of them. *Mr. Holland's Opus* is a tribute to her and everyone else in her grand profession."

The movie is the story of Glenn Holland (played by Richard Dreyfuss), a young musician who desires to make it to the big time as a composer. But when money gets tight and he needs to take care of his family, he reluctantly seeks employment as a teacher. That job, which he takes only on a temporary basis, becomes his life. Through the course of the movie, he discovers that he wants to share his love for music with his students, and in the process he discovers himself.

The pivotal point of the movie comes when Mr. Holland's teaching position is eliminated because of cutbacks, and he suddenly realizes he has reached middle age. In that moment, he knows that he has forever missed his chance to pull up roots, go to New York, and take his symphony with him, which he has been writing in his spare moments for over twenty years. Despondent and feeling rejected, he believes he has wasted his life.

He is depressed and on the verge of bitterness as he ambles dejectedly down the hall, preparing to walk out of the school for the last time. That's when he hears something in the auditorium. When he checks to see what it is, he discovers hundreds of cheering students whose lives he changed during all his years of teaching. That group even includes the governor of the state, whose life took a major turn for the better under his mentoring.

The director of the movie, Stephen Herek, was attracted to *Mr. Holland's Opus* because the screenplay touched him. "It made me cry," he admitted. "Very rarely do I read something where I actually end up with tears flowing freely. But that's how I felt at the end of [the script]. The story makes a hero out of Everyman who happens to be a teacher. . . . It's also a story about how one human being can affect a lot of other people and touch their lives in a very special way."

Many people believe that touching the lives of others can be done only by some elite group of specially gifted people. But that's not the case. Any ordinary person—just like Glenn Holland in the movie—can make a positive impact on the lives of others.

— from *Failing Forward*

Every life needs a purpose to which
it can give the energies of its mind
and the enthusiasm of its heart.

———— " ————

Start by doing what's necessary;
then do what's possible; and
suddenly you are doing the impossible.

— ST. FRANCIS OF ASSISI

———— " ————

No individual has any right to come into
the world and go out of it without leaving
behind him distinct and legitimate reasons
for having passed through it.

— GEORGE WASHINGTON CARVER

> **"**

until a man is nothing,
God can make nothing out of him.

— MARTIN LUTHER

> **"**

The purpose of life is not to be happy.
The purpose of life is to matter,
to be productive, to have it make some
difference that you lived at all.
Happiness, in the ancient, noble verse,
means self-fulfillment and is given to those who
use to the fullest whatever talents
God or luck or fate bestowed upon them.

— LEO ROSTEN

we GO where our DREAMS take us.

NO PLACE FOR EGO

DURING THE CIVIL WAR, President Abraham Lincoln
faced not only the weariness of trying to bring together a
divided nation, but also intense political pressure. Under such
pressure Lincoln signed an order to transfer a regiment from
one field of battle to another.

When Lincoln's Secretary of War, Edwin M. Stanton, found
out about it, he refused to carry out his commander-in-chief's
directive. "Lincoln is a fool for ever signing the orders," he said.

A man preoccupied with success would have been infuriated.
But not Lincoln. He knew that the preservation of the Union
was a cause of much greater significance than his personal
success. Lincoln said simply, "If Stanton said I'm a fool, then
I must be one. He is nearly always right in military matters.
I'll step over and find out what his reasoning is."

After Lincoln listened to Stanton's views, he rescinded the order,
saving thousands of lives and avoiding a military disaster.

True heroism is remarkably sober,
very undramatic. It is not the urge to surpass
all others at whatever cost, but the urge
to serve others at whatever the cost.

— ARTHUR ASHE

———————| " |———————

Talent is God-given—BE HUMBLE.
Fame is man-given—BE THANKFUL.
Conceit is self-given—BE CAREFUL.

— AUTHOR UNKNOWN

———————| " |———————

Do not follow where the path may lead.
Follow God, instead, where there is no path
and leave a trail.

There is no magic in small plans.
when I consider my ministry,
I think of the world. Anything less
than that would not be worthy
of Christ nor of His will for my life.

— HENRIETTA MEARS

we all live under the same sky,
but we don't all have the same horizon.

— KONRAD ADENAUER

Don't go to your grave with a life unused.

— BOBBY BOWDEN

WHAT'S YOUR MOTIVE?

YOU CAN'T MAKE THE JOURNEY from success to significance unless you have checked your motives to make sure they're pure. If you're only out to improve yourself and your situation, then you're still on the success track.

Having the right motives makes it possible to change tracks. The right motives . . .

1. KEEP YOU FROM MANIPULATING PEOPLE

2. STRENGTHEN YOU DURING ADVERSITY

3. GIVE YOU CREDIBILITY WITH OTHERS

4. ALLOW YOU TO SERVE OTHERS

5. OPEN YOU UP TO THE FAVOR OF GOD

You and I live in an age when only
a rare minority of individuals desire
to spend their lives in pursuit of objectives
which are bigger than they are. In our age,
for most people, when they die
it will be as though they never lived.

— RUSTY RUSTENBACH

———————— " ————————

I am only one, but I am one. I cannot do everything,
but I can do something. And that which I can do,
by the grace of God, I will do.

— DWIGHT L. MOODY

———————— " ————————

The real test of a man is not when he plays the role
that he wants for himself,
but when he plays the role destiny has for him.

— SØREN KIERKEGAARD

NO DO-OVERS

ANTHONY CAMPOLO HAS RECOUNTED a sociological study in which fifty people in their late nineties were asked one question: If you could live your life over again, what would you do differently? It was an open-ended question allowing any kind of response, yet three answers kept surfacing from the people:

1. IF I HAD IT TO DO OVER AGAIN, I WOULD REFLECT MORE.

2. IF I HAD IT TO DO OVER AGAIN, I WOULD RISK MORE.

3. IF I HAD IT TO DO OVER AGAIN, I WOULD DO MORE THINGS THAT WOULD LIVE ON AFTER I AM DEAD.

What a perfect description of the preparation for significance! These near centenarians didn't miss any of the traditional trappings of success. They didn't wish for more money, power, or fame. They wanted to get beyond themselves and do something that mattered, boldly and purposefully. They recognized the value of a life given to significance.

AS RESPONSIBILITY IS PASSED TO YOUR HANDS, it will not do, as you live the rest of your life, to assume that someone else will bear the major burdens, that someone else will demonstrate the key convictions, that someone else will run for office, that someone else will take care of the poor, that someone else will visit the sick, protect civil rights, enforce the law, preserve culture, transmit value, maintain civilization, and defend freedom.

You must never forget that what you do not value will not be valued, that what you do not remember will not be remembered, that what you do not change will not be changed, that what you do not do will not be done. You can, if you will, craft a society whose leaders, business and political, are less obsessed with the need for money. It is not really a question of what to do but simply the will to do it.

— ALEXANDER M. SAUNDERS, JR.

GROW
BEYOND
YOURSELF

By IMPROVING yourself,
the world is made BETTER.

The moment you stop learning,
you stop leading.

— RICK WARREN

You will never find out what you can do
until you do all you can to find out.

— JOHN C. MAXWELL

HOW DO YOU MEASURE
SIGNIFICANCE?

THE PEOPLE WHO MET HENRY would have called him
anything but successful. He attended a good Ivy League
school, but after that he never seemed to stick with much
of anything. Immediately after graduation, he took a
position as a teacher. But he soon resigned because he didn't
approve of the way the administration handled disciplinary
issues with the students. The next year he helped his brother
start a small private school, but when his brother became
sick, he didn't have the ability to sustain it, so the school
was closed.

Occasionally Henry worked in his family's factory, but he
had no desire to make a career of it. He liked writing in a
journal, something he started while in school. He dabbled
in poetry. And every now and then, he got something he
wrote into a small journal published by some friends.

When a friend worked it out for him to get a job as a
private tutor for a wealthy family on Staten Island in New
York, Henry took it.

But that lasted for only two years. So Henry went back to his hometown, and the friend who had gotten him the tutoring job let him stay in a shack on his property. Later, the friend let him live in his house as a kind of handyman. After that, Henry moved back home, even though he was in his thirties.

For the next decade or so, Henry traveled a little, he spoke out concerning social causes, and he got a few pieces of his writing published. In his last years, he worked on his journals, hoping that maybe someday they would be published. He died of tuberculosis in his mid forties.

LEAVING NO MARK

Though he never married and didn't seem to make much of a mark on the world, he was always very passionate. He once refused to pay a tax as a war protest, and it landed him in jail. When a friend asked him, "What are you doing in jail?" Henry's glib response was, "What are you doing out of jail?" He was irritated that his aunt paid his tax and he was let out of jail after only one day.

Henry's protest didn't do anything to change the government's policies concerning the war, but it did help to galvanize some of his ideas and prompted him to put them into writing. He called his essay "Resistance to Civil Government." In case you haven't already guessed it, Henry's full name was Henry David Thoureau, his essay was later renamed "Civil Disobedience," and the friend who sponsored him and visited him in jail was none other than Ralph Waldo Emerson.

Thoreau didn't have much to show for his years on earth. He didn't fight any great battles, lead any great movements, or create any great organizations. What he did is keep growing, keep learning, keep working to improve himself. His search to grow beyond himself never ended. And the result of that growth came to fruition in his writings, most of which were published after his death.

Thoreau's essay on civil disobedience, which was published in 1849 (thirteen years before his death), is considered a masterpiece today. "Under a government which imprisons any unjustly," wrote Thoreau in his essay, "the true place for a just man is also in prison . . . the only house in a slave State in which a free man can abide with honor."

ON SECOND THOUGHT...

Thomas Carlyle called "Civil Disobedience" the one truly original American contribution to western civilization. More importantly, its ideas made a lasting impact on the world. Fifty years after Thoreau wrote his essay, Mohandas Gandhi, India's greatest leader, was inspired by Thoreau's ideas on civil disobedience. And it set him on a course of action that led to India's independence from British rule. One hundred years after Thoreau's death, Martin Luther King, Jr., based his practices for advancing civil rights on the words of Thoreau and the courageous example of Gandhi.

Significance is much more difficult to measure than success. How do you judge the impact of a person's life? Do you base it on the quality of one life touched or on the quantity of lives influenced? And at what time do you try to make the measurement? By the time the person is 40, 65, or 90? Does history make the judgment—at 10, 100, or 1,000 years after a person is gone? Or will we know the answer only in heaven?

No individual can measure his or her own impact. So what is one to do? Keep growing. Do something every day to make yourself better able to give. Whatever talents, skills, and resources you have, improve them to the point that people benefit from the overflow of your life. Then keep giving. And let God worry about keeping score.

there is a theory of human behavior

that says people subconsciously retard

their own intellectual growth.

They come to rely on cliches and habits.

once they reach the age of

their own personal comfort with the world,

they stop learning and their mind runs on idle

for the rest of their days.

They may progress organizationally,

they may be ambitious and eager,

and they may even work night and day.

But they learn no more.

— PHILIP B. CROSBY

There are some people that if they don't know,

you can't tell them.

— LOUIS ARMSTRONG

It is the capacity to develop and
improve their skills that distinguishes leaders
from their followers.

— WARREN BENNIS & BERT NANUS

❝

The most important question to ask
yourself on the job isn't "what am I getting?"
but "what am I becoming?"

❞

It is not the fast tempo of modern life
that kills but the boredom,
a lack of strong interest
and failure to grow that destroy.
It is the feeling that nothing is worthwhile
that makes men ill and unhappy.

— HAROLD W. DODDS

If we don't change, we don't grow.

If we don't grow, we are not really living.

Growth demands a temporary surrender

of security. It may mean a giving up

of familiar but limiting patterns,

safe but unrewarding work,

values no longer believed in,

relationships that have lost their meaning.

As Dostoevsky put it, 'Taking a new step,

uttering a new word is what people fear most.'

The real fear should be the opposite course.

– GAIL SHEEHY

We must be the change

we wish to see in the world.

– MAHATMA GANDHI

WHY NOT TODAY?

IT'S SAID THAT THE ROMAN SCHOLAR CATO began to study Greek when he was over 80 years old. When he was asked why he was tackling such a difficult task at his age, he responded, "It's the earliest age I have left."

What difficult task stands between you and your calling to significance? Are you putting it off? Or are you working at achieving it? Forget about excuses and get started. The longer you wait, the more you delay making your most significant contribution!

"

I am willing to put myself through anything;
temporary pain or discomfort means nothing to me
as long as I can see that the experience will take me
to a new level. I am interested in the unknown,
and the only path to the unknown is through
breaking barriers, an often-painful process.

— DIANA NYAD

"

Leaders set the pace
as learners and teachers.

—JOHN C. MAXWELL

—— | " | ——

Not everything that is faced can be changed.
But nothing can be changed until it is faced.

—JAMES BALDWIN

—— | " | ——

Within you right now is the power
to do things you never dreamed possible.
This power becomes available to you
as soon as you change your beliefs.

—MAXWELL MALTZ

SETTING THE COURSE FOR SIGNIFICANT GROWTH

The mere desire to grow and reach your potential isn't enough to empower you to make a significant contribution in the world. You need more:

1.   ATTITUDE — Knowing How to Feel

I once read in the *Cox Report on American Business* that 94 percent of all Forbes 500 executives attributed their success more to attitude than to any other ingredient. If you believe you can grow to your potential, that opens the door to continual self improvement.

2.   PRIORITIES — Knowing How to Choose

You cannot develop to your highest potential in every area of life; a jack of all trades is a master of none. You need to make choices about where you will grow. Focus on your strengths. The greatest leaders do only a few things exceptionally well.

3. VISION — KNOWING HOW TO SEE

Vision is seeing things as God wants them to be.
If your vision is born out of God's desires, you will
always be on track.

4. DIRECTION — KNOWING HOW TO BEGIN

Vince Abner observed, "Vision isn't enough—it must
be combined with venture. It is not enough to stare up
the steps; we must step up the stairs." To move from
desire to action, plan your first steps. Then get going.

5. CREATIVITY — KNOWING HOW TO THINK

Growth is a journey, and on any journey you will
encounter unforeseen obstacles. Your ability to
overcome these barriers will determine whether
you succeed.

6.   RESPONSIBILITY—KNOWING HOW TO FINISH

Growth does not come easily. It takes complete dedication, a
whatever-it-takes mindset, and the determination to give your
very best effort. Give it your all, and you will get all that
you can out of it.

we cannot achieve our wildest dreams
by remaining who we are.

—JOHN   C.   MAXWELL

If we don't change the direction we're going,
we're likely to end up where we are headed.

– CHINESE PROVERB

——| " |——

Take responsibility for your own development.

——| " |——

our business in life is not
to get ahead of others,
but to get ahead of ourselves—
to break our own records,
to outstrip our yesterday by our today,
to do our work with more force
than ever before.

– STEWARD B. JOHNSON

STRETCH TO SIGNIFICANCE

IF YOU WANT TO STRETCH from success to significance, then you will have to stretch yourself. No one ever achieved anything significant without becoming better as an individual. It's the only way one can become equal to the great challenges of life.

Stretching doesn't come naturally. You need to work at it. Know this:

1. MOST PEOPLE AVOID STRETCHING.

2. MOST PEOPLE WANT TO BE MOTIVATED BEFORE STRETCHING.

3. MOST PEOPLE FEEL VULNERABLE WHEN THEY STRETCH.

4. MOST PEOPLE NEED AFFIRMATION TO KEEP STRETCHING.

5. MOST PEOPLE DON'T REALIZE THAT THE NEED TO STRETCH NEVER ENDS.

6. MOST PEOPLE LOOK BACK AT STRETCHING EXPERIENCES AS THEIR FINEST HOURS.

7. THE FEW WHO STRETCH ALL THEIR LIVES INSPIRE FUTURE GENERATIONS.

If you're ready to stretch, then discover, dedicate, and develop your potential. And get out of your comfort zone and stay there.

one doesn't discover new lands
without consenting to lose sight
of the shore for a very long time.

— ANDRE GIDE

———————— " ————————

There is a price to pay to grow.
commitment is the price.

— ED COLE

———————— " ————————

The greatest of all miracles is that
we need not be tomorrow what we are today,
but we can improve if we make use of
the potentials implanted in us by God.

— SAMUEL M. SILVER

God never puts anyone in a place too small to grow

or too unimportant to make a difference.

— JOHN C. MAXWELL

unless you try to do something

beyond what you have already mastered,

you will never grow.

— RONALD E. OSBORN

PEOPLE CHANGE WHEN THEY...

HURT ENOUGH that they have to

LEARN ENOUGH that they want to

RECEIVE ENOUGH that they are able to

Beware of endeavoring
to become a great man in a hurry.
one such attempt in ten thousand
may succeed.
These are fearful odds.

—BENJAMIN DISRAELI

No matter how far you have gone
on a wrong road, turn back.

—TURKISH PROVERB

GET OUT OF YOUR
COMFORT ZONE

PEOPLE CANNOT DO SOMETHING of significance and stay in their comfort zones at the same time. To do something great, you must take risks.

There are many reasons people cruise along in their comfort zones instead of trying to fight their way into the end zone. Here are ten:

1. LACK OF HUNGER: Poet Rudyard Kipling said, "If you don't get what you want, it is a sign that you did not seriously want it, or that you tried to bargain over the price."

2. UNWILLINGNESS TO SACRIFICE: When you begin thinking you can get something for nothing, you find it harder and harder to do something.

3. LACK OF CONFIDENCE: "I don't think I can" comes from "I don't think I am."

4. STRUGGLING WITH PERSONAL ISSUES: People have a hard time "taking off" when they're weighed down by a lot of emotional baggage.

5. TOO MUCH TIME SPENT ON TRIVIA: Activity is not necessarily accomplishment. Don't keep busy doing busy work.

6. LACK OF CREATIVITY: Tom Hirshfield observed, "If you don't ask 'why this?' often enough, somebody will ask 'why you?'"

7. LIVING OFF YESTERDAY: If the past looks great to you, then you probably haven't done enough today.

8. LACK OF FOCUS: The main thing is to keep the main thing the main thing.

9. PAST FAILURES: Just because you have failed in the past doesn't mean *you* are a failure.

10. PHYSICAL, EMOTIONAL, OR SPIRITUAL EXHAUSTION: Sometimes you just need to set aside time to rest and regroup. That can energize you to start anew or to refresh your passion for a previous vision.

The life of every man

is a diary in which

he means to

write one story

and writes another;

and his humblest hour

is when he compares

the volume as it is

with what he hoped

to make it.

— J. M. BARRIE

GIVE
BEYOND
YOURSELF

LIFE'S most persistent
and urgent QUESTION is,
'WHAT are you doing
for OTHERS?'

— MARTIN LUTHER KING, JR.

MAXWELL'S MAXIMS ON MONEY

I'VE YET TO MEET A PERSON who moved from success to significance who didn't have the right attitude toward money. If you love money or possessions more than you love people, then you will have a hard time achieving significance.

Here are five observations about money that describe the philosophy I've adopted toward it:

1. THE BEST DECISIONS ARE BASED ON POTENTIAL, NOT DOLLARS.

2. INSTEAD OF TRYING TO MAKE DOLLARS FROM PEOPLE, IT'S BETTER TO TRY TO ADD VALUE TO PEOPLE.

3. MONEY FLOWS TO WHERE NEEDS ARE BEING MET.

4. THE ONLY REAL VALUE OF MONEY IS THAT IT GIVES OPTIONS.

5. THE TEST OF GOOD STEWARDSHIP IS WHAT YOU DO WITH THE MONEY YOU'VE ALREADY RECEIVED.

HE is the richest man

in the esteem of the world

who has gotten most.

HE is the richest man

in the esteem of heaven

who has given most.

— F. B. MEYER

HE who wishes to secure

the good of others has

already secured his own.

— CONFUCIUS

If you do what you can,

with what you have, where you are,

then God won't leave you

where you are and He will increase

what you have.

— BILL PURVIS

——— " ———

You are not here merely to make a living.

You are here in order to enable the world to live more

amply, with greater vision, with a finer spirit of hope

and achievement. You are here to enrich the world, and

you impoverish yourself if you forget the errand.

— WOODROW WILSON

——— " ———

Serious battle calls for commitment

rather than interest.

— LARRY MITCHELL

GOING FROM ORDINARY TO EXTRAORDINARY

HOW MANY AVERAGE PEOPLE ever achieve something of significance? Perhaps there's a better way to ask that question: Can anyone whose highest aspiration is merely average do something extraordinary? I believe the answer is no. Ordinary people can do extraordinary things— only if they are willing to give something extra. To make a significant impact, you need . . .

1. A LITTLE EXTRA EFFORT: John Wooden said, "Doing your best is more than being the best." If "good enough" is good enough, you'll never be good enough.

2. A LITTLE EXTRA TIME: Peter Lowe said, "The most common trait I have found in all successful people is that they have conquered the temptation to give up." If that is true of people who achieve success, how much more important it is for people who desire significance.

George Button said, "Genius is nothing but a greater aptitude for patience."

3. A LITTLE EXTRA HELP: There are two sure ways to disaster—taking everybody's advice and taking nobody's advice. Your quest for significance must come from within. You can't find it by consensus. However, you can't go it alone either. You need the advice of experienced people who can help you.

4. A LITTLE EXTRA REALISM: Max De Pree advises, "The first responsibility of a leader is to define reality." Leaders must have vision for what *could be*, but they must also look hard at what *really is*.

5. A LITTLE EXTRA CHANGE: Most people don't change because they see the light. They do it only when they feel the heat. But as a leader, if you are already feeling the heat, it's too late to make a change. Leaders must be ready, willing, and able to change before anyone else. And the first change they must be ready to make is in themselves.

6. A LITTLE EXTRA THINKING: Earl Nightingale said, "You are, and you become, what you think about." If that's true, then you need to spend more time thinking, because it will determine not only your effectiveness but also your identity.

7. A LITTLE EXTRA PLANNING: It's true that planning is beneficial for anyone. But it's essential for leaders. What they do impacts everyone on their team. And what they model is emulated by their people. So how should you plan? Cardiologist Robert Eliot suggests the following: "It's important to run not on the fast track, but on *your* track. Pretend you have only six months to live, and make three lists: the things you *have* to do, *want* to do, and neither have to do nor want to do. Then for the rest of your life, forget everything on the third list."

whatever you have received more than others—

in health, in talents, in ability, in success,

in a pleasant childhood, in harmonious conditions

of home life—all this you must not take to yourself

as a matter of course. In gratitude for your

good fortune, you must render some sacrifice

of your own life for another life.

— ALBERT SCHWEITZER

Heart is what separates

the good from the great.

— MICHAEL JORDAN

He who scatters sunshine

will have light and warmth and cheer

even when his own sun has set.

The person who lives in fear
of giving away too much
often finds what he has kept for
himself is too little to live upon.

– UNKNOWN

———— | " | ————

Give not from the top of your purse
but from the bottom of your heart.

———— | " | ————

The service we render to others is really
the rent we pay for our room on this earth.
It is obvious that man is himself a traveler;
that the purpose of this world is not
'to have and to hold' but 'to give and serve.'
There can be no other meaning.

– SIR WILFRED T. GRENFELL

After the cheers have died and the stadium is empty,

after the headlines have been written and after

you are back in the quiet of your own room and

the super Bowl ring has been placed on the dresser

and all the pomp and fanfare has faded,

the enduring thing that is left is the dedication

to doing with our lives the very best we can to make

the world a better place in which to live.

— V I N C E   L O M B A R D I

No man can live happily

who regards himself alone,

who turns everything

to his own advantage.

You must live for others if you

wish to live for yourself.

— S E N E C A

what we have done for ourselves

alone dies with us.

what we have done for others

and the world remains and

is immortal.

— ALBERT PIKE

There is one who scatters, yet increases more;

and there is one who witholds more than is right,

but it leads to poverty.

The generous soul will be made rich,

and he who waters will also be watered himself.

— PROVERBS 11:24,25

we make a living by what we get,
but we make a life by what we give.

—WINSTON CHURCHILL

"

no man becomes rich
unless he enriches others.

—ANDREW CARNEGIE

"

giving is a joy if we do it in the right spirit.
it all depends on whether we think of it as
"what can i spare?" or as "what can i share?"

—ESTHER YORK BURKHOLDER

some people treat life like a slot machine,

trying to put in as little as possible,

and always hoping to hit the jackpot.

But I believe that people are wiser, happier,

and have more inner peace

when they think of life as a solid,

intelligent investment from which

they receive in terms of what they put in.

— ROGER HULL

———— " ————

All getting separates you from others;

all giving unites to others.

— ST. FRANCIS OF ASSISI

———— " ————

once we make the decision

to give of ourselves,

God will provide the opportunity.

we cannot hold a torch

to light another's path

without brightening our own.

— BEN SWEETLAND

The only gift is a portion of thyself.

— RALPH WALDO EMERSON

we exist temporarily

through what we take,

but we live forever

through what we give.

— DOUGLAS M. LAWSON

INVENTING IMPACT

WHEN DEAN KAMEN WAS FIVE years old, he used to wake up his father, a professional illustrator, in the middle of the night to draw pictures of ideas he had gotten. Kamen has never been short on ideas. At age 15, he decided to put one of his concepts into concrete form. Using a few hundred dollars of stock electronic components, he built a control board for light and sound shows.

"It was the first electronic, fully automated board that replaced the need for a dozen men working switches and levers in an auditorium," says Kamen. He sold it for several thousand dollars to the Hayden Planetarium at New York City's Museum of Natural History.[1] The next year, Kamen quit his summer job to manufacture the boards and sold dozens of them. It made the high school student a lot of money. He spent much of it to improve his home workshop so that he could keep inventing.

FLASH FORWARD TO THE PRESENT

TODAY, IN HIS EARLY FIFTIES, Kamen is a multimillionaire. And thanks to his recent invention, the Segway, the self-balancing, pollution-free, two-wheeled personal transport, he has become famous. Kamen has been called "America's greatest living inventor" and the "Pied Piper of technology." He holds more than 150 patents, has received several honorary doctorates, and has been honored with numerous awards, including the National Medal of Technology from the President of the United States. Few people could claim greater success than Kamen.

But success is not what Dean Kamen is after.

"If you want your life to matter," observes Kamen, "no consumer product can be as important as a medical advance, even one that most people never hear about."[2]

Kamen began to focus on technical solutions to medical problems when he was in college, thanks in part to his brother. "I was looking for something else to work on. And my brother, who was then in medical school, explained to me that there was no automatic pump designed to inject medication into very young patients—infants and small children," says Kamen. "So I started working with miniature pumps and timers, and in a few months I had come up with AutoSyringe."[3]

The device dispenses medicine in precise doses so that people such as juvenile cancer patients won't need to be confined to hospitals and doctor's offices for treatment. Later, Kamen developed an insulin pump for diabetics using similar technology. He then created a portable, affordable dialysis machine for kidney patients, which he says "gave tens of thousands of people dignity and mobility and personal independence."[4] He also created a stint used in heart patients and a twenty-first century wheelchair called IBot, capable of climbing stairs and raising its driver up to a standing person's eye level.

Kamen's inventions keep making a positive impact on people's lives—and keep getting him recognition. In addition to the National Medal of Technology, he has received the Kilby Award, which celebrates those who make extraordinary contributions to society; the Heinz Award in Technology, the Economy and Employment; the Lemelson-MIT prize for inventors; and he was elected to the National Academy of Engineering.

PASSING ON HIS GIFT

WHILE KAMEN WORKS TO CREATE devices that improve lives, he is also trying to prepare the next generation to do the same. He does that by promoting science in schools. In 1985, he established Science Enrichment Encounters, a hands-on science museum for children in Manchester, N.H. And later he founded U.S. FIRST (For Inspiration and Recognition of Science and Technology), the organization that he calls his "most important invention." It unites engineering teams from business and universities with high-school students in an annual robot design and construction contest. For younger children he's even added a junior robotic competition using Legos.

And of course, he's still thinking and inventing. "Every morning is an exciting new day in which I try to keep up and I try to contribute," says Kamen. "But I'm just one little guy with one little company, and we're trying as hard as we can."[5] Kamen is proof that one person with a heart for significance can make an incredible impact on others.

spread love everywhere you go;

first of all in your own house.

Give love to your children,

to your wife or husband,

to a next door neighbor. . . .

Let no one ever come to you

without leaving better and happier.

Be the living expression of God's kindness;

kindness in your face,

kindness in your eyes,

kindness in your smile,

kindness in your warm greeting.

— MOTHER TERESA

HE who waits to do a
great deal of good at once
will never do anything.

– SAMUEL JOHNSON

———| " |———

MOST people feel best about themselves
when they give their best
to something greater than themselves.

– JOHN C. MAXWELL

———| " |———

YOU have not lived today
until you have done something for someone
who can never repay you.

– JOHN BUNYAN

HER MOST PRECIOUS GIFT

IN THE EARLY 1950S, a young woman named Elisabeth left the United States with a group of missionaries to Ecuador with the hope of reaching the Quichua Indians. In that group was a young man named Jim Elliot, who had been courting her since 1947. While working together and giving their lives to serving the Ecuadoran Indians, they finally decided to give themselves to each by getting married.

After they had been together about two years and had a ten-month-old daughter named Valerie, Jim and four other missionaries felt compelled to make contact with another small group of Indians living in an area called the Auca. These Indians had a fierce reputation. The earliest record of contact with them was of their killing a priest in the 1600s. Since then, they had attacked every outsider who came their way. Even the other Ecuadoran Indians avoided them because of their brutality.

As Jim and the others prepared to make contact, Elisabeth knew the five men would be putting themselves in danger, but she was resolute. The couple had given their lives to this mission. For several weeks, a missionary pilot flew a small plane over an Aucan village and dropped supplies and other items as gifts. They even included pictures of themselves to prepare the Aucans for a first meeting.

A few weeks later, Jim and four others landed on a small stretch of beach on the Curaray River and set up camp. There they made contact with three Aucans—a man and two women—who seemed to be friendly and receptive. And in following days, they met with several others. They told their wives by radio that it looked like they were making significant progress in befriending the tribe.

But then a few days later, the men failed to check in with the base camp at an appointed time. Their wives waited in vain to hear from them. Minutes passed, then hours, and then a day. Elisabeth and the others feared the worst.

A search party went out to look for the men and radioed back bad news. They had spotted the body of a white man floating in the river. Eventually, one by one, the searchers found the men. With each it was the same: they had been slashed with Aucan spears. All five of the men were dead.

Under those circumstances, many people in Elisabeth Elliot's shoes would have gone home. It's one thing to be willing to give up a comfortable life in the United States to help other people; it's quite another to give the life of your spouse. But Elliot had a truly generous heart. Despite her terrible loss, she still wanted to help the people of Ecuador. She stayed and served the Quichuans with whom she was living.

But what happened next is even more remarkable. Other missionaries continued trying to connect with that Aucan village. And after a couple of years they succeeded. Immediately Elisabeth Elliot rushed to the village. Was it for revenge? No, it was to work with the people there and serve them. Elliot lived and worked among the Aucan people for two years, and many of them gladly accepted the message of God's love she carried—including two of the seven men who had killed her husband.

That happened because she and others understood that to do something of significance, you have to give beyond yourself.

— from *The 21 Indispensable Qualities of a Leader*

Everybody can be great . . . because
anybody can serve. You don't have to have
a college degree to serve. You don't have
to make your subject and your verb agree
to serve. You only need a heart full of grace.
A soul generated by love.

— MARTIN LUTHER KING, JR.

I know God will not give me anything
I can't handle. I just wish
that He didn't trust me so much.

— MOTHER TERESA

Most people are too insecure
to give anything away.

— KEVIN MYERS

GATHER

BEYOND

YOURSELF

people need a VISION,
but a vision needs PEOPLE too.
you can have a VISION
to do something SIGNIFICANT,
but if NOBODY buys into it,
you don't have ANYTHING.

—JOHN C. MAXWELL

CREATING POSITIVE CHANGE

TO DO GREAT THINGS, you need to create an environment for your team where change is encouraged. That way your people will always find the best solutions for the challenges they face. How do you create a climate for change? You need four elements:

TRUST — the more people trust their leader, the more they will change.

SUCCESS — the more successful the organization becomes, the more they will change.

CONFIDENCE — the more confidence that the leader exhibits, the more they will change.

OPENNESS — The more open the leader is about failures, the more they will change.

Over the years I've learned a lot about coaching staffs,
and one piece of advice I would pass on to a young
coach—or a corporation executive or even a band
president—is this: Don't make them in your image.
Don't even try. My assistants don't look alike,
think alike, or have the same personalities.
And I sure don't want them all thinking the way I do.
You don't strive for sameness, you strive for balance.

—PAUL "BEAR" BRYANT

The way you follow sets the pattern
for your leadership. You cannot take
short cuts in the way you follow
and expect trust from those you lead.
Your people will do what they see.

A team is two or more people
with two things in common: a shared goal
and good communication.

— CHUCK BOWMAN

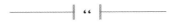

There are no problems
we cannot solve together,
and very few that we can solve
by ourselves.

— LYNDON BAINES JOHNSON

Those closest to you will

stretch your vision

or choke your dreams.

— JOHN C. MAXWELL

——————| " |——————

It marks a big step

on your development

when you come to realize

that other people can help

you do a better job

than you could do alone.

— ANDREW CARNEGIE

——————| " |——————

If I had it to do all over again,

I'd get help.

if you make it to the top alone,
then you didn't climb a very high hill.

—JOHN C. MAXWELL

there is something more powerful
than anybody—and that is everybody.

—EDDY RICKENBACKER

WINNING THE TOUGH ONE

IN 1972 I WAS FACED WITH a very difficult situation. I was
moving to Lancaster, Ohio, where I would be taking over the
leadership of a church. Before I accepted the position, I found
out from a friend that the church had just gone through a big
battle related to a building project. Heading up one of the
factions was the number one influencer in the church, a man
named Jim.

Because the previous senior pastor had butted heads with Jim
more than a few times, I knew my best chance for being
successful in leadership there was to connect with Jim. So the
first thing I did when I arrived was make an appointment to
meet him in my office.

Jim was a big man. He was about six feet four inches and
weighed about 250 pounds — the kind of guy who could
go bear hunting with nothing but a switch. He was very
intimidating, and he was about 65 years old. I, on the other
hand, was only 25. When he came in, I said, "Jim, I know
you're the influencer in this church, and I want you to know
that I've decided that I'm going to do everything in my power
to build a good relationship with you. I'd like to meet with

you every Tuesday for lunch to talk through issues. While I'm the leader here, I'll never take any decision to the people without first discussing it with you. I really want to work with you.

"But I also want you to know that I've heard you're a very negative person," I said, "and that you like to fight battles. If you decide to work against me, I guess we'll just have to be on opposite sides. And because you have so much influence, I know you'll win most of the time in the beginning. But I'm going to develop relationships with people and draw new people to this church, and someday, I'll have greater influence than you.

"But I don't want to battle you," I continued. "You're 65 years old; let's say you've got another 10 to 15 years of good health and productivity ahead of you. If you want, you can make these years be your very best and make your life count. We can do a lot of great things together at this church, but the decision is yours."

When I got finished, Jim didn't say a word. He got up from his seat, walked into the hall, and stopped to take a drink at the water fountain. I followed him out and waited. After a long time, he stood up straight and turned around.

And when he did, I could see that tears were rolling down his cheeks. And then he gave me a great big bear hug and said, "You can count on me to be on your side."

And Jim did get on my side. As it turned out, he did live about another ten years, and because he was willing to help, we accomplished some great things together at that church. But it never would have happened if I hadn't had the courage to try to make a connection with him that first day in my office.

Never underestimate the power of building relationships with people before asking them to follow you. Effective leaders know that you first have to touch people's hearts before you ask them for a hand.

— from *The 21 Indispensable Qualities of a Leader*

FIVE QUESTIONS FOR BUILDING
A SIGNIFICANT TEAM

1. **CALLING:** What is our focus?

2. **CHEMISTRY:** Who are the right people?

3. **CULTURE:** How do we develop leaders?

4. **CHALLENGE:** Where are we headed?

5. **CALENDAR:** When do we start?

Talk about purpose and people
will listen, but to get them to follow,
you must act with purpose.

—LORIN WOOLFE

It's not how heavy the load is—
it's how you carry it.

A significant vision is a picture
of the future that produces passion
in people.

—JOHN C. MAXWELL

ONCE YOU FIND THEM . . . HOW TO LEAD THEM

LEADERSHIP OF A TEAM is the highest expression of servant leadership. This is true because team leadership embodies each of the principles of servant leadership:

- You must humble yourself in order to build a team. Humility allows you to see the need for others. Pride insists on working alone.

- You cannot seek a position and have the team succeed. Following Jesus keeps you on mission and out of competition with others.

- You must be willing to give up your personal right to be served and find greatness in service to the mission and the other team members.

- You must trust that God is in control of your life in order to risk service to those on the team.

- You must take up the towel of service to meet the needs of the group.

- You must share both responsibility and authority with team members in order to meet the greater need of the team's goal.

- You must multiply your leadership by empowering other members of the team to lead.

— C. GENE WILKES (from *Jesus on Leadership*)

we should not only use

all the brains we have,

but all that we can borrow.

— W O O D R O W   W I L S O N

———————‖ " ‖———————

None of us is as strong

as all of us.

———————‖ " ‖———————

you can buy a man's time; you can buy

his physical presence at a given place;

you can even buy a measured number

of his skilled muscular motions per hour.

But you can not buy enthusiasm . . .

you can not buy loyalty . . .

you can not buy the devotion of hearts,

minds or souls. you must earn these.

— C L A R E N C E   F R A N C I S

I am a self-made man,

but I think if I had to

do it over again, I would

call in someone else.

—ROLLAND YOUNG

significant leaders

know the way,

go the way,

and show the way.

—JOHN C. MAXWELL

SOME JUST CAN'T SEE IT

SOMETIMES EVEN AN ACCOMPLISHED leader with a compelling vision has trouble getting everyone to buy into his dreams. That was true in the early 1950s when a friend of television pioneer Art Linkletter tried to convince him to buy some land. His buddy, a movie executive who had been a close family friend for years, drove him out into the country to look at some property. After driving for more than twenty-five miles, they turned off the main road and drove through fields and groves of trees. There wasn't a person for miles. They saw grazing horses and the occasional abandoned shed.

Art's friend began explaining his next bold venture, an amusement park unlike anything the world had ever seen. It would be its own little world, and it would contain areas with names like "Fantasyland" and "Tomorrowland." Art's friend said it would be called Disneyland.

Art Linkletter thought his friend Walt Disney was crazy. *Who in the world is going to drive twenty-five miles to ride a roller coaster?* he thought to himself. Linkletter later wrote, "I had such admiration for his business acumen and his show-business savvy that I hardly knew how to tell him I thought he was making the biggest, most ruinous mistake of his entire life."[6]

After painting a verbal picture of his vision, Disney said to Linkletter, "Art, financially I can handle only Disneyland itself. It will take everything I have as it is. But the land bordering on it, where we're standing now, will be jammed with hotels and motels and restaurants and convention halls to accommodate the people who will come to spend their entire vacations here at my park in just a couple of years. I've bought all I can afford. And I want you to have an opportunity to get some of the surrounding acreage because it will increase in value several hundred times in the next five years."

Walt Disney had no agenda with his friend other than to add value to him. He wanted to share an opportunity. But Linkletter just couldn't see it. He made excuses and said he would look into it later.

"Later will be too late," responded Disney. "You had better move on it right now."[7]

Disney was right, of course. And Linkletter never forgot his walk back to the car because he later figured that it probably cost him about a million dollars per step.

Art Linkletter and Walt Disney never let this incident get in the way of their friendship. They remained close up until Walt's death.

As you seek to enlist people into the fulfillment of your vision, don't be discouraged when people can't see what you do. And don't despair if people you respect won't take the trip with you—even if you're inviting them to do it for their own benefit. Celebrate when people choose to join you. And keep loving those who don't. That, too, is significant.

GO
BEYOND
YOURSELF

You shouldn't GLOAT
about anything you've done;
you ought to KEEP GOING
and try to find something
better to do.

—DAVID PACKARD

None of us knows

when we will die.

But any one of us,

if we wish,

may select

our own epitaph.

— JOHN C. MAXWELL

people of significance take joy

in helping others succeed.

THEIR LOVE WILL GO ON AND ON

IN 1914, A SHIP SUFFERED A COLLISION and sustained
a rip in her hull off the American coast. Quickly she began
filling with sea water and in a matter of minutes sank. There
were 1,477 people on board. Tragically, 1,012 lost their lives.

No, the ship was not the *Titanic*. She was *Empress of Ireland*,
a vessel that had set out from Quebec, Canada, and was
headed for Liverpool, England. And she didn't strike an
iceberg. Headed out of the Saint Lawrence River toward
the North Atlantic Ocean on a foggy May night, she
received a glancing blow from the Norwegian ship *Storstad*.
The impact was described as "deceptively gentle." However,
the *Storstad*'s bow, which was reinforced to break through ice,
was said to have "gone between the liner's steel ribs as
smoothly as an assassin's knife."[8] In ten minutes, *The Empress
of Ireland* lay on her side. Four minutes later, her hull
disappeared under the frigid water's surface. More people
lost their lives than during the sinking of the *Titanic*.

It is a sad story that's not well known because her sinking occurred only a few months before the outbreak of World War I and because the ship didn't have the luxury or famous passenger list of the *Titanic.* But a remarkable thing happened on the *Empress of Ireland* that night. The ship carried 840 passengers, 170 of whom were Salvation Army workers headed for a convention in London.

Since the 1860s, the Salvation Army has been known for its tireless service. Its members continually "go beyond themselves," by helping the poorest and neediest people in society. Most of the Salvation Army officers aboard *Empress of Ireland* didn't survive the tragedy. Why? Because as the ship sank and they noticed that others didn't have life belts, they gave their own away. Survivors recounted how many of the officers strapped the devices on other passengers saying, "I know Jesus, so I can die better than you can."[9] And with that, they performed one final heroic act of service.

—— " ——

DO all the good you can,

BY all the means you can,

IN all the ways you can,

IN all the places you can,

AT all the times you can,

TO all the people you can,

AS long as ever you can.

—JOHN WESLEY

—— " ——

every golden era in human history

proceeds from the devotion

and righteous passion

of some single individual.

There are no bona fide

mass movements;

it just looks that way.

There is always one man

who knows his God and

knows where he is going.

— RICHARD E. DAY

—————| " |—————

As long as you believe that

you are doing something meaningful,

you can go forward.

—————| " |—————

A leader discovers the hidden chasm

between where things are

and where things would better be,

and strings up a makeshift bridge

to attempt the crossing.

From the other side he guides

those who dare to cross his

rickety traverse until the engineers

can build a sturdier span for all.

— MEL ZIEGLER

The individual succumbs,

but he does not die

if he has left something behind.

— WILL DURANT

SEPARATING SIGNIFICANCE FROM SUCCESS

IF YOU WANT TO KNOW whether you're ready to go beyond yourself and make the leap from success to significance, check yourself in three areas:

MOTIVES:

The motivation for success is usually selfish.

The motivation for significance cannot be selfish.

INFLUENCE:

With success, your influence is limited.

With significance, your influence becomes unlimited.

TIME:

Success can last no more than a lifetime.

Significance will last beyond your lifetime.

Humility comes when

a leader sees himself

in the light of the task

he desires to achieve.

—JOHN C. MAXWELL

———————| " |————— —

Make no small plans

for they have no capacity

to stir men's souls.

———————| " |—————————

Most of the things worth doing

in this life had been declared impossible

by others before they were done.

—JOHN C. MAXWELL

Big thinking precedes

great achievement.

— WILFERD A. PETERSON

———| " |———

You have never tested

God's resources until you have

attempted the impossible.

———| " |———

A rock pile ceases to be a rock pile

the moment a single man contemplates it,

bearing within him the image of a cathedral.

— ANTOINE DE SAINT-EXUPERY

I think most of us are looking for a challenge,
not a job. Most of us, like the assembly line worker,
have jobs that are too small for our spirit.
Jobs are not big enough for people.

— NORA WATSON

THE MOMENT YOU RESOLVE to take hold of life with all
your might and make the most of yourself at any cost, to
sacrifice all lesser ambitions to your one great aim, to cut
loose from everything that interferes with this aim, to stand
alone, firm in your purpose, whatever happens, you set in
motion the divine inner forces the Creator has implanted in
you for your own development. Live up to your resolve,
work as the Creator meant you to work for the perfecting
of His plan and you will be invincible. No power on earth
can hold you back from success.

— ORISON SWETT MARDEN

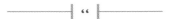

The final test of a leader
is that he leaves behind in other people
the convictions and the will to carry on.

—WALTER LIPPMANN

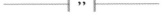

A leader is one
who sees more than others see,
who sees farther than others see,
and who sees before others see.

—LEROY EIMS

WHAT IS YOUR VALUE?

To get an idea of whether you are adding value to others, ask yourself these five questions:

1. WOULD THOSE WHO WORK WITH YOU CONFIRM THAT YOU ADD VALUE TO THEM?

2. DO YOUR IDEAS AND PLANS DIRECTLY IMPACT THE MISSION OF THE ORGANIZATION IN A POSITIVE WAY?

3. ARE YOU WORTH MUCH MORE THAN YOUR SALARY?

4. DO THOSE OVER YOU CONSTANTLY AFFIRM YOUR VALUE TO THE ORGANIZATION?

5. DO YOU DO WHATEVER IT TAKES TO ADD VALUE TO YOUR LEADER, YOUR EMPLOYEES, AND THE ORGANIZATION?

Nobody who ever gave

his best regretted it.

— GEORGE HALAS

—— " ——

If there is a way to do it better,

find it.

— THOMAS A. EDISON

—— " ——

Half of knowing what you want

is knowing what you must give up

before you get it.

— SIDNEY HOWARD

the master in the art of living makes
little distinction between his work and his play,
his labor and his leisure, his mind and his body,
his information and his recreation,
his love and his religion. He hardly knows
which is which. He simply pursues his vision
of excellence at whatever he does,
leaving others to decide whether he is working or
playing. To him he's always doing both.

— JAMES MICHENER

Hold yourself responsible for a higher standard
than anybody else expects of you.

— HENRY WARD BEECHER

The quality of a person's life
is in direct proportion to their commitment
to excellence, regardless of their
chosen field of endeavor.

– VINCENT T. LOMBARDI

—— " ——

Our real freedom comes from
being aware that we do not
have to save the world,
merely make a difference
in the place where we live.

– PARKER PALMER

—— " ——

Great men undertake great things
because they are great;
fools because they think them easy.

– VAUVENARGUES

THE SHAPE OF SIGNIFICANCE

A LIFE OF SIGNIFICANCE does not look the same for every person. Each is as individual as the person who lives it. They come in many shapes and sizes. However, there are some things that all people who achieve significance have in common:

THEY STRIVE FOR EXCELLENCE.

THEY DO THE SMALL THINGS WELL.

THEY CARE ABOUT OTHERS.

THEY CONSTANTLY IMPROVE THEMSELVES.

THEY GIVE IT THEIR ALL.

"

You will invest your life
in something, or you will
throw it away on nothing.

— HADDON ROBINSON

"

we can be marked from the past
or we can make a mark on the future.

– J . C . WATTS

———— ❝ ————

you haven't been given life
to test the waters.
you're here to make waves.

– JOHN C. MAXWELL

———— ❞ ————

we have made at least a start
in discovering the meaning in human life
when we plant shade trees under which
we know full well we will never sit.

– ELTON TRUEBLOOD

DON'T REST ON YOUR SUCCESS

WHEN PEOPLE WHO MAKE SUCCESS their goal achieve it,
they become tempted to stop and rest there. They've reached
the top of their personal mountain. They've set their record.
They've captured their holy grail. In a way, they die before
their time.

People who go beyond themselves and their own goals, who
desire significance, never rest on their laurels. Their quest is
never done. No matter how much good they do, there are
always opportunities for more.

If you've achieved success and you've been resting, then it's
time to get back into the game. Keep going as long as . . .

YOUR DREAMS ARE NOT FULFILLED,

YOU HAVE AN ANSWER TO A NEED, OR

YOU HAVE NOT REACHED YOUR POTENTIAL.

—— " ——

when you were born,

you cried and the world rejoiced.

Live your life in such a manner

that when you die

the world cries and you rejoice.

—— " ——

He who has done his best

for his own time

has lived for all times.

—JOHANN VON SCHILLER

A life isn't significant except
for its impact on other lives.

— JACKIE ROBINSON

If the whole world followed you,
would it be a better world?

The serene, silent beauty
of a holy life is the most
powerful influence in the world,
next to the might of God.

— BLAISE PASCAL

Life is a great big canvas
and you should throw all the
paint on it that you can.

– DANNY KAYE

when I die, rest assured that people
will know that I lived a full life.
Live in such a way that your friends
and family will say the same of you.

– JOHN C. MAXWELL

SUCCESS CAME WITH SIGNIFICANCE

HE'S ONE OF THE GREATEST TEAM builders in all of sports, yet you've probably never heard of him. Take a look at these impressive accomplishments:

- 40 Consecutive Basketball Seasons with at Least 20 Wins
- 5 National Championships
- #1 Ranking in his Region in 20 of the Last 33 Years
- Lifetime Winning Percentage of .870

His name is Morgan Wootten. And why have most people never heard of him? Because he is a high school basketball coach!

John Wooden, the greatest college basketball coach of all time and who led the UCLA Bruins, said of Wootten:

"People say Morgan Wootten is the best high school coach in the country. I disagree. I know of no finer coach at any level—high school, college or pro. I've said it elsewhere and I'll say it here: I stand in awe of him."[10]

That's a pretty strong recommendation from the man who won ten NCAA national championships and coached some of the most talented players in the game, including Kareem Abdul-Jabbar. (By the way, when Jabbar was in high school, his team lost only one game—to Morgan Wootten's team!)

CALLED TO SIGNFICANCE

MORGAN WOOTTEN NEVER PLANNED to coach a team. But when he was a nineteen-year-old college student, a friend tricked him into accepting a job coaching kids from an orphanage in baseball, a game he knew little about. The team had no uniforms and no equipment. And despite working hard, they lost all sixteen of their games.

During that first season, Wootten fell in love with those kids. When they asked him to coach football, he couldn't refuse them. Besides, he had played football in high school, so he knew something about it. The orphanage team went undefeated and won the Washington, D.C., CYO championship. But more importantly, Wootten began to realize that he wanted to invest his life in children.

Even that first year he began making a difference in the lives of kids. He remembers one boy in particular who had started stealing and kept being brought back to the orphanage by the police. Wootten took the boy under his wing. Wootten recalled:

"We started spending some time together. I took him to my house and he'd enjoy Mom's meals. He spent weekends with us. He became friends with my brother and sisters. He's still in Washington today and doing quite well and known to a lot of people. Anyone would be proud to call him their son. He was bound for a life of crime and jail, however, and maybe a lot worse, until someone gave him the greatest gift a parent can give a child—his time."

Giving of himself to the people on his teams is something Wootten has done every year since then. Virginia Military Institute coach Marty Fletcher, a former player and assistant under Wooten, summarized his talent this way: "His secret is that he makes whomever he is with feel like the most important person in the world."[11]

CREATING A DYNASTY

BEFORE LONG WOOTTEN WAS INVITED to become an assistant coach at a local powerhouse school. Then in 1956 with a couple of years experience under his belt, he became head coach at DeMatha High School. Wootten was taking over a bunch of losing teams. He called together all the students who wanted to play sports at DeMatha, and he told them:

"Fellas, things are going to change. I know how bad DeMatha's teams have been during these last few years, but that's over with. We're going to win at DeMatha and we're going to build a tradition of winning. Starting right now. . . . But let me tell you how we're going to do it. We're going to outwork every team we ever play . . . . With a lot of hard work and discipline and dedication, people are going to hear about us and respect us, because DeMatha will be a winner."[12]

That year, the football team won half of its games, which was quite an accomplishment. In basketball and baseball, they were division champions. His teams have been winning ever since. DeMatha has long been considered a dynasty.

On October 13, 2000, Wootten was inducted into the Naismith Basketball Hall of Fame in Springfield, Massachusetts. At that time, his teams had amassed a record of 1,210-183. Over the years, more than 250 of his players have won college scholarships. Twelve players from his high school teams went on to play in the NBA.[13]

IT'S NOT ABOUT BASKETBALL

BUT WINNING GAMES AND HONORS isn't what excites Wootten most. It's investing in the kids. Wootten says:

"Coaches at every level have a tendency to lose sight of their purpose at times, especially after success arrives. They start to put the cart before the horse by working harder and harder to develop their teams, using their boys or girls to do it, gradually forgetting that their real purpose should be to develop the kids, using their teams to do it."[14]

Wootten's attitude reaps rewards not only for a team, but for the individuals on the team.

For example, for a twenty-six-year stretch, *every single one of Wootten's seniors earned college scholarships*—not just starters but bench players too. Penn State assistant coach Chuck Swenson observed, "Even if you know a kid isn't a great player, if he's a DeMatha player, he'll help your program. With Morgan, you know you're getting a quality kid who will make good grades and work hard for you."[15] Gary Williams, head coach of the University of Maryland said, "His players are so fundamentally sound, do so many things right, that they may not improve as much as kids in another program who haven't been as well coached. . . . These aren't raw talents; they're refined ones."[16] What's remarkable is that this is being said of high school students, not college players or pros.

Morgan Wootten invests in his players because it is the right thing to do, because he cares about them. That practice has made his players good, his teams successful, and his career remarkable. It's true that he is the first basketball coach to have won 1,200 games at any level, but that is not what makes his life significant. That comes from the investment he has made in people.

—From *The 17 Indisputable Laws of Teamwork*

LAST THOUGHTS ON SIGNIFICANCE

As you pursue significance for your life, keep these thoughts in mind:

1. THE JOURNEY TO SIGNIFICANCE TAKES TIME.

2. SUCCESS IS USUALLY THE STEPPING STONE TO SIGNIFICANCE.

3. PURSUING SIGNIFICANCE WILL TAKE YOU OUT OF YOUR COMFORT ZONE.

4. ONCE YOU TASTE SIGNIFICANCE, SUCCESS WILL NEVER SATISFY YOU AGAIN.

ACKNOWLEDGEMENTS

Grateful acknowledgement is made to the following publishers for permission to reprint this copyrighted material.

John C. Maxwell, *Failing Forward*
(Nashville: Thomas Nelson, 2000). Used by permission.

John. C. Maxwell, *The 17 Indisputable Laws of Teamwork*
(Nashville: Thomas Nelson, 2001). Used by permission.

John C. Maxwell, *The 21 Indispensable Qualities of a Leader*
(Nashville: Thomas Nelson, 1999). Used by permission.

John C. Maxwell, *The 21 Irrefutable Laws of Leadership*
(Nashville: Thomas Nelson, 2002). Used by permission.

C. Gene Wilkes, *Jesus on Leadership*
(Carol Stream, IL: Tyndale House Publishers, 1998), 212. Used by permission.

Every effort has been made to locate sources of all quoted material. If any acknowledgment has been overlooked, it is inadvertent.

---

1. Matthew McCann Fenton, "America's Greatest Living Inventor," Biography, October 2003, 74.

2. Ibid, 76.

3. Ibid.

4. Ibid.

5. Ibid, 91.

6. Art Linkletter, Yes, You Can! (New York: Simon and Schuster, 1979), 248.

7. Ibid.

8. Quoted from Lost Liners in "Empress of Ireland," www.pbs.org/lostliners/empress.html, 31 October 2003.

9. Dennis J. DeHaan, Windows on the Word (Grand Rapids: Baker Book House, 1984) 36.

10. Don Banks, "Teacher First, Seldom Second, Wooten has Built Monument to Excellence at Maryland's DeMatha High," St. Petersburg Times, 3 April 1987, www.dematha.org.

11. John Meinstein, "A Down-to-Earth Coach Brings DeMatha to New Heights," Washington Post, 27 February 1984, www.dematha.org.

12. Morgan Wootten and Bill Gilbert, From Orphans to Champions: The Story of DeMatha's Morgan Wootten (New York: Antheneum, 1979), 24-25.

13. William Plummer, "Wootten's Way," People, 20 November 2000, 166.

14. Wooten and Gilbert, From Orphans to Champions, 12-13.

15. Feinstein, A Down-to-Earth Coach.

16. Ibid.

"well done good and faithful SERVANT
you have been FAITHFUL
over a FEW things,
I will make you RULER
over MANY things.
enter into the JOY of the LORD."

— MATTHEW 25:23